I0530921

Your Story
God's Story

Johnny L. Edwards Jr.

Your Story
God's Story

Published by Krystal Lee Enterprises (KLE Publishing)
Copyright © 2025 by Johnny L Edwards Jr. All rights reserved. Please send comments and questions:

Krystal Lee Enterprises
770-240-0089 Ext. 1
sales@KLEPub.com

To Reach the Author:
Email: yourstories777@gmail.com

Cover Design: Rayven Baker - ImageRé

All scripture verses were accessed and cited from BibleHub.com

Printed in the United States of America.
All rights reserved. No part of this book may be reproduced or transmitted in any form or by any means, electronic or mechanical, including photocopying, recording, or any information storage and retrieval system without written permission of the publisher except for brief quotations used in reviews, written specifically for inclusion in a newspaper, blog, magazine, or academic paper.

ISBN: 979-8-89987-903-6

Acknowledgements

This book is dedicated, first to my Lord Jesus Christ who preordained my destiny before the foundation of the world. I also want to thank my amazing wife, Katrina, who never lost faith in my ability to finish this project. She believed in me, even during my moments of doubt. I acknowledge my sons, Chris, Johnathan, Joshua, and James, along with their families. I also want to thank my sister Monique for her listening ear and my older sister Marilyn, whose devotion to Jesus inspired me to write this book

Your Story God's Story

Table of Contents

Introduction

While writing this book, I had the honor of being the eulogist at my sister's funeral. She lived a life that reflected a close relationship and commitment to Jesus Christ. She was a woman of faith who desired to share Christ's love with her family and community.

Her greatest wish was to love and serve Him. Like all great stories, my sister's story has an ending. She knew her walk with Jesus would lead her into a new story and final resting place in His presence. Like my sister, we all have a story. I wrote this book to ask, "What's your story?

If you enjoy reading, you have probably read great inspirational books. I personally love science fiction; it stretches my imagination. There are many book genres, and we all have different tastes, but the most incredible story is the story of your life.

I'm not referring to a biography written by someone else after you're gone or an autobiography you have penned. I'm talking about the present moment you are experiencing right now. Did you know that you fill the pages of your life daily, and every action and decision you make adds a new chapter to your epic? Your story is unique and essential; it matters to God and the world.

Second Corinthians 3:2 says, "You yourselves are our letter, written on our hearts, known and read by everyone" (NIV).

The Apostle Paul recognized that others were observing his life and conduct. Who you are and what you do in life truly matter. Everyone you encounter, including family, friends, co-workers, and strangers, read your life and story. Every day and every passing moment adds pages to your narrative.

So, what is the theme of your story right now? What are they reading? What does your story say about you? Does it inspire them? Does your story reflect hope or defeat? How is your life impacting their narrative?

Most importantly, how is your story affecting you? I believe God is very interested in our stories—how they are written and lived, especially how they conclude. He has archived all our stories in His heavenly library and will review them with us on the day of judgment.

Revelations 20:12 says, "I saw the dead, both great and small, standing before God's throne. And the books were opened, including the Book of Life. And the dead were judged according to what they had done, as recorded in the books" (NLT).

God will review and reflect on your story at the end of your life. The most significant theme in your narrative should embody God's will for you. Did you incorporate Him into your story?

Let's read what the Bible says about this. Ecclesiastes 12:13-14 says, "(13) Now all has been heard; here is the conclusion of the matter: Fear God and keep his commandments, for this is the duty of all mankind. (14) For God will bring every deed into judgment, including every hidden thing, whether it is good or evil" (NIV).

Every life is a book that God will read and judge. What's your story? Your story has the potential to be a beautiful narrative of faith, hope, and love that inspires others and glorifies God, and you get to write your story. So, "What's your story?"

Chapter 1
God Is On Your Side

Believe it or not, God enjoys a happy ending. I grew up believing God was waiting to catch you if you didn't line up. As a child, I knew I wasn't always doing what was right, and from my limited understanding of God, I might have been on His list of those needing improvement.

I remember that one of my biggest fears in elementary school was getting in trouble and going to the principal's office. I don't know about you, but the principal represented a picture of divine judgment for me. With just one word, I could receive detention, suspension, or be expelled from school, much like how God cast Adam and Eve out of the garden.

Unfortunately, as we enter adulthood, we sometimes see God as that school principal waiting in his office, eager to pass judgment on anyone who breaks the rules, and ready to turn our happily ever after into a tragedy. We make God the villain in our story, but nothing could be further from the truth.

Psalm 145:8 says, "The LORD is gracious, and full of compassion; slow to anger, and of great mercy" (KJV).

God is not angry with you and is not waiting to punish you at the first chance. The Bible reveals that He is loving, patient, and merciful. He is committed to making our lives a success story. There was a time in the Old Testament when God's people were not following His plan for them, which led them into captivity in a city called Babylon. In the book of Jeremiah, chapter twenty-nine, God unveils His plan to restore His people.

Jeremiah 29:10-11 says, "(10) This is what the LORD says: 'When seventy years are completed for Babylon, I will come to you and fulfill my good promise to bring you back to this place. (11) For I know the plans I have for you," declares the LORD, "plans to prosper you and not to harm you, plans to give you hope and a future" (NIV).

You may wonder why God would care about my story when I feel broken and messed up and have made wrong choices in life, and am now suffering the consequences. Through God's grace and mercy, you can receive a second chance. Fortunately, He recognizes that challenging times can overwhelm us, causing us to make unwise choices.

You see, you set the tone for your story. Israel's disobedience to God's instructions resulted in a period of captivity in their narrative. God is so gracious that even when you stray, if you return to Him, He will restore you to a success story filled with hope and a future.

The most important step is to keep God as part of your story. You should never hide from God. I remember when I was a child; if I brought home a poor report card or did something wrong, I thought my parents would be upset and disappointed. I would try to hide it from them because I feared getting into trouble and thought they would stop loving me.

Fortunately, our God is not like human parents, who may sometimes be disappointed by our actions. Guess what? You can't surprise or disappoint God! That's right! He knows everything about us and our flaws; He has prepared a success story as our Savior and entered heaven to guide us on our journey.

Hebrews 4:13-16 says, "(13) Nothing in all creation is hidden from God. Everything is naked and exposed before his eyes, and he is the one to whom we are accountable. (14) So then, since we have a great High Priest who has entered heaven, Jesus the Son of God, let us hold firmly to what we believe. (15) This High Priest of ours understands our weaknesses, for he faced all of the same testings we do, yet he did not sin. (16) So let us come boldly to the throne of our gracious God. There we will receive his mercy, and we will find grace to help us when we need it most" (NLT).

Hallelujah! Our God knows all about us, and He is on our side!

Chapter 2
God Is With You

God has revealed in Scripture that He will guide you in creating a success story. You cannot accomplish this without His help. Psalms 37:23-24 says, "(23) The LORD directs the steps of the godly. He delights in every detail of their lives. (24) Though they stumble, they will never fall, for the LORD holds them by the hand" (NLT).

Wow! God loves you so much that He will help you as you write your story. You have the free will to shape your narrative, but must follow God's guidelines. Straying from God's plan may not be beneficial to you. You will be led by your flesh (the carnal side) or your spirit (the part of you that hears and connects with God).

Proverbs 14:12 says, "There is a path before each person that seems right, but it ends in death" (NLT). This scripture means that your choices can negatively affect your story, as every decision has consequences. God supports you by providing wisdom, particularly during crucial decisions.

James 1:5 says, "If you need wisdom, ask our generous God, and he will give it to you. He will not rebuke you for asking" (NLT). God wants you to seek Him for wisdom and guidance because He has the answers to all of life's challenges. I understand that, in the past, you were accustomed to rushing ahead of God and then asking Him, "God bless this mess," but we don't have to live that way anymore. God makes it clear that He provides everything to you when you seek Him first.

Matthew 6:33 says, "Seek the Kingdom of God above all else, and live righteously, and he will give you everything you need" (NLT). This is a promise from God to you: if you seek His direction and guidance for your life and submit to His plan, you will find purpose and fulfillment in every part of your life. But first, you must surrender to God's plan! Jesus said, "Except a man be born again, he cannot see the Kingdom of God" (John 3:3, KJV). Building a relationship with Jesus Christ is essential before you can truly live your story.

Being born again is crucial for renewing your spirit and experiencing new life in God. It means inviting Jesus Christ into your heart as your personal Savior and Lord. If you're ready to be born again, pray this prayer to accept Jesus as your Savior:

"Dear Heavenly Father, I come to you in the name of Jesus. I acknowledge that I am a sinner; forgive me of my sins. I believe Jesus shed his precious blood to give me a new life. Romans 10:9 says, 'If I confess with my mouth, 'Jesus is Lord,' and believe in my heart that God raised him from the dead, then I will be saved."

I confess Jesus Christ right now as Lord of my life and believe in my heart that God raised him from the dead for my salvation. I now commit my life to you. Fill me with your Holy Spirit so that I can fulfill my purpose and destiny in you. Amen!"

If you prayed this prayer with faith, truly believing every word, then you are now born again into God's kingdom! You have received eternal life through Christ. He will guide your journey toward a glorious future. It is amazing to know that God wants to be part of your story. God considers you His masterpiece and His handiwork.

Ephesians 2:10 says, "For we are God's masterpiece. He has created us anew in Christ Jesus, so we can do the good things he planned for us long ago" (NLT).

God created you with a purpose, and now

is the time to dream anew to discover the paths that will fulfill your story. Remember, God is always with you!

Chapter 3
Live Your Dream

Have you ever had amazing dreams like becoming your favorite superhero or achieving incredible things as a child? These God-given dreams serve as a gentle reminder that our stories are meant for greatness, and perhaps we were wonderfully created to accomplish something truly special and meaningful. It's time to pursue your dreams.

Sometimes, life's experiences can prevent you from pursuing your dreams. Sadly, struggles and setbacks are also part of life. Dreams play a vital role in shaping your story, I can say with confidence, and with God's help, anything can be achieved.

Psalms 37:23 says, "The LORD directs the steps of the godly. He delights in every detail of their lives" (NLT).

You don't need to settle for mediocrity when God has revealed a greater purpose for your life. Through my Bible studies, I have learned that God can speak to us through dreams. In the Old Testament, a young man named Joseph was given a dream by God that revealed His divine plan for him. Many people in the Bible were guided by their dreams. Our divinely inspired dreams remind us of the importance of our own stories. The Apostle Paul understood this when he wrote to the Ephesian church.

Ephesians 4:1 says, "Therefore I, a prisoner for serving the Lord, beg you to lead a life worthy of your calling, for you have been called by God" (NLT).

I previously mentioned Jeremiah 29, where God tells us that He has plans to prosper and not harm us. This indicates there is an expected outcome for your life and story. God placed a purpose on your life before you were born, and the dreams He gave you are meant to help fulfill that purpose.

If you've ever wondered why you're naturally good at something, maybe it's God's gift to help you complete your story. Sometimes, God gives you dreams and talents to inspire you to follow His will for your life. Dreams can sometimes reveal a greater purpose and meaning in life.

Therefore, Satan often tries to distract us from realizing the amazing dreams that God has in store for us. God believes in our potential and has provided us with all the tools and resources we need to succeed. Remember, He also gave us free will, so we have the wonderful opportunity to choose whether to follow His guidance. While many people may choose to follow Satan through their choices and actions, it's always encouraging to remember that we have the power to choose a different path and walk in God's loving plan.

Joshua 24:15 says, "But if serving the LORD seems undesirable to you, then choose for yourselves this day whom you will serve..." (NIV).

For those of you who dream and choose to follow God's path for your life, stay focused and don't accept anything less than God's best for you. The secret is to prioritize God's will for your story above all other desires. Matthew 6:33 says, "But seek ye first the kingdom of God, and his righteousness; and all these things shall be added unto you" (KJV).

Chapter 4
Prioritize Your Story

What you value, you should prioritize by putting it first. Important things you want to accomplish in your day, you likewise, do first so they don't fall by the wayside. Similar to decisions you make in the natural, how you respond in the spirit also matters. Please keep in mind that your understanding and response to the next verse will influence how your story turns out.

Ecclesiastes 12:13-14 says, "(13) Let us hear the conclusion of the whole matter: Fear God, and keep his commandments: for this is the whole duty of man. (14) For God shall bring every work into judgment, with every secret thing, whether it be good, or whether it be evil" (KJV).

This statement is attributed to King Solomon of Israel, known as the wisest man who ever lived. He was not only the wisest person on earth but also recognized as the wealthiest man in history. Solomon's wisdom and wealth were granted by God because of his desire to follow God's will (1 Kings 3:5-14).

As a king and someone born into royalty, King Solomon enjoyed a life filled with luxury and abundance. Throughout his reign, he lacked for nothing, yet by the end of his life, Solomon showed us that true happiness and peace don't come from material wealth or possessions. In the book of Ecclesiastes, which he authored, Solomon shares his reflections on life and what truly matters.

As he approached the later years of his life, he took time to reevaluate his journey and realized that some of his priorities had been misplaced. He understood that every decision he made carried lasting, eternal significance. Solomon wrote these words in Proverbs 14:12, "There is a way which seemeth right unto a man, but the end thereof are the ways of death" (KJV).

I believe King Solomon had a wake-up call. As he looked back on his life, he saw that chasing only selfish, worldly possessions leads to a life focused on self-gratification. This path causes you to miss out on fulfilling your true purpose and ultimately forces you to answer for your choices before God. Your life is meant to obey and serve Him, as He has a greater and more meaningful story for you than anyone could imagine.

Proverbs 19:21 says, "Many are the plans in a person's heart, but it is the LORD's purpose that prevails" (NIV).

Our stories are connected to Him, and Solomon realized that the most lasting things in life are those that relate to God. Ecclesiastes 1:14 says, "I have seen all the works that are done under the sun; and, behold, all is vanity and vexation of spirit" (KJV). I believe Solomon understood before his death that all the wealth in the world couldn't provide true satisfaction or contentment; it simply couldn't replace God's plan and story for his life.

Your story's purpose is found in the God who created you. His wonderful plan is for us, His family, to be with Him forever. We believe that His will will be done on earth just as it is in heaven (Matthew 6:9-10). God's heart is to restore everything that was lost when Adam and Eve disobeyed in the Garden of Eden, whether in Heaven or on Earth. This, dear readers, is the beautiful story we are part of!

Ephesians 1:9-10 says this: "(9) Having made known unto us the mystery of his will, according to his good pleasure which he hath purposed in himself: (10) That in the dispensation of the fullness of times he might gather together in one all things in Christ, both which are in heaven, and which are on earth; even in him..." (KJV).

God has a beautiful and inspiring plan for each of us. It's so important to really prioritize following His story and plan for our lives. His story helps us return to our true purpose and destiny. Remember, we are all fearfully and wonderfully made by Him, which makes us truly special.

Chapter 5
Your Happy Ending

Everyone enjoys a happy ending to stories, and this is something God also cherishes. That's why making God a central part of your story is so important. How you choose to conclude your life's story should truly matter to you. As Ecclesiastes 7:8 reminds us, "Better is the end of a thing than the beginning thereof: and the patient in spirit is better than the proud in spirit" (KJV).

We have the opportunity, by God's grace, to adopt His theme for our stories by making Him first in our lives. Jesus is coming back, and we will be judged on our faith and obedience to God. 2 Corinthians 5:10 says, "For we must all appear before the judgment seat of Christ, so that each of us may receive what is due us for the things done while in the body, whether good or bad" (NIV).

When we stand before Jesus, we will receive a spiritual "book review" that evaluates our acceptable and unacceptable words, thoughts, actions, conduct, and performances. Every aspect will be examined and judged as either worthy or unworthy. Therefore, the conclusion of our story holds immense significance.

Are you looking forward to receiving the crown of life with Jesus Christ in the Kingdom of God? Have you been walking in faith and obediently following God's Word? When you stand before Jesus, will you be able to proudly say that His story is your story and you've pursued and fulfilled the purpose He has given you? Remember, the Lord loves to see us succeed, and He eagerly wants to celebrate with us when we meet Him.

Matthew 25:21 says, "His lord said unto him, Well done, thou good and faithful servant: thou hast been faithful over a few things, I will make thee ruler over many things: enter thou into the joy of thy lord" (KJV).

There will be great blessings for those who love God and pursue His will for their lives. Many believe that God is the antagonist in their story; on the contrary, He is the hero in all our stories, on the scene, saving us through His Son Jesus Christ, and preserving us in our time of need. His presence in our lives gives us hope and a future. God does have a "happy ending" planned out for your life if you desire Him.

Psalms 16:11 says, "You make known to me the path of life; you will fill me with joy in your presence, with eternal pleasures at your right hand" (NIV).

You must understand that your entire life has been about getting God back in your story so you can enter into a glorious new story in His kingdom!

Chapter 6
Your New Story

I began this book to celebrate my sister's life, who has transitioned to be with the Lord. She inspired me with her dedication to serving God and has entered a magnificent new story. God has promised you a future filled with new stories in a glorious new world.

Revelations 21:1 says, "And I saw a new heaven and a new earth: for the first heaven and the first earth were passed away; and there was no more sea" (KJV).

This begins a new start for all of God's creation.

Revelations 21:5 says, "And he that sat upon the throne said, Behold, I make all things new. And he said unto me, Write: for these words are true and faithful" (KJV).

God has promised you that there will be much more to your story in His kingdom. The

Spirit of God reveals to us this fact.

1 Cor. 2:9-10 says, "(9) But as it is written, Eye hath not seen, nor ear heard, neither have entered into the heart of man, the things which God hath prepared for them that love him. (10) But God hath revealed them unto us by his Spirit: for the Spirit searcheth all things, yea, the deep things of God" (KJV).

It's exciting to think about more wonders awaiting us in the future. Can you imagine a world free from evil and sin's influence? Our new story places you and me right in the presence of God.

John 14:2-3 says, "(2) In my Father's house are many mansions: if it were not so, I would have told you. I go to prepare a place for you. (3) And if I go and prepare a place for you, I will come again, and receive you unto myself; that where I am, there ye may be also (KJV).

Are you ready to start a new story and direction in your life? Remember these key points:

- God is on your side, playing the hero in your story, not the villain.

- He is dedicated to turning your life into a success story.

- Remember, God is with you when

you invite Him into your story. Accept Jesus into your life today.

- Dreams from God inspire you to go beyond mediocrity.

- Make His plans a priority for you and include Him in your story.

- Everyone loves a happy ending, and God does too.

- A new story with God awaits you in His house.

In conclusion, your story shapes your future. This book reminds you that you are responsible for everything that happens within the pages of your life story. God clearly shows His desire for your success by encouraging you to include Him in your story.

So, when your journey ends at the end of your life, you can look forward to sharing an exciting new chapter in the eternal kingdom of our God and Savior, Jesus Christ. My final question to you is: Is "Your Story" actually God's Story?

SCAN ME

Call or Text:
770-240-0089 Press Extension 1
Web: KLEpub.com
Email Services@klepub.com

It's time to start and finish **YOUR Story!**

KLE Publishing specializes in helping people become authors. In as little as 15 to 90 days, we can help you develop your books and e-books and publish to 39,000 outlets! We also offer audiobook services.

Write, Edit, Format, Publish
We can help from
Start to Finish.

Explore and learn more about published authors affiliated with KLE.

 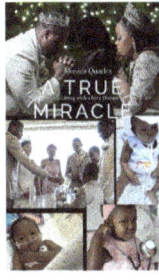   

KLEPub.com

www.ingramcontent.com/pod-product-compliance
Lightning Source LLC
Chambersburg PA
CBHW071227130626
46555CB00004B/1881